AF131433

BOOK ANALYSIS

By Alba Díez de Ure

Strangers on a Train

by Patricia Highsmith

PATRICIA HIGHSMITH

AMERICAN NOVELIST

- **Born in Fort Worth in 1921.**
- **Died in Locarno in 1995.**
- **Notable works:**
  - *The Price of Salt* (1952), novel
  - *The Talented Mr. Ripley* (1955), novel
  - *A Dog's Ransom* (1972), novel

Patricia Highsmith was one of the most important thriller and mystery writers of the 20th century. Her work explores the psychological underpinnings behind criminal minds and investigates the philosophical questions behind crime, including the notions of good and evil.

A number of her novels explore the personalities of criminals and seek to uncover how a person can deviate far enough from social norms to become a murderer.

Highsmith wrote 22 novels and several short story collections and essays, and her works have been adapted numerous times for the cinema and the theatre. She first rose to fame after Alfred Hitchcock (1899-1980) adapted her novel *Strangers on a Train* in 1951, and her career spanned five decades. One of her most important works is the Ripley series, commonly known as the "Ripliad", which started with *The Talented Mr. Ripley* and follows the life of a charming con artist and serial killer.

In her personal life, Highsmith was known for her hostile manners and reclusive character. Throughout her life, Highsmith had alcohol abuse problems and suffered from cyclical depression, as well as a number of other physical and mental conditions.

STRANGERS ON A TRAIN

TWO LIVES ENTANGLED BY MURDER

- **Genre:** novel
- **Reference edition:** Highsmith, P. (1988) *Strangers on a Train*. London: Penguin Books.
- **1st edition:** 1950
- **Themes:** morality, chance encounters, duality, predestination, manipulation

Strangers on a Train was Patricia Highsmith's first novel and the work that started her successful career as a psychological thriller writer. The novel explores notions of good and evil by entangling the lives of two men after a brief encounter on a train.

In the novel, a psychopathic young man named Charles Anthony Bruno meets architect Guy Haines on a train journey. After a short introduction and conversation, Bruno suggests exchanging murders: he will kill Guy's wife if Haines will kill Bruno's father. This way, both men will get rid of people who are bothering them and move on with their lives.

According to Bruno, this is a perfect crime: they will never be caught if the police is not able to find a connection between the two men. However, Guy's sense of guilt and Bruno's obsession with Guy eventually give away their responsibility for the crimes.

The novel enjoyed modest success at the time it was published, and only became popular a year later, when director Alfred Hitchcock produced his movie adaptation.

SUMMARY

THE PLOTTING OF A MURDER

Architect Guy Haines is travelling by train to Metcalf, where he hopes to end his marriage to Miriam, who has been unfaithful to him. Guy's reputation as an architect is flourishing and he wants to settle his divorce to marry his true love, Anne Faulkner.

Guy is interrupted by Charles Anthony Bruno, a confident young man who is going on holiday to his mother's home in Santa Fe. Bruno introduces himself and insists on having dinner with Guy. Reluctantly, Guy accepts.

As dinner progresses, both men become inebriated and Bruno, who talks about his hatred of his father, seems increasingly interested in Guy's life. Bruno ends up asking Guy if he has ever thought of murdering someone. Guy responds negatively but Bruno frantically insists on a suggestion: to exchange murders. Bruno will kill Guy's wife and, in exchange, Guy will have to kill Bruno's father. According to Bruno, it will be a perfect crime: the police will not suspect either of them as they are unrelated to their respective victims. Guy feels extremely uncomfortable at Bruno's suggestion and ends dinner, leaving the book he had been reading in Bruno's train compartment.

The next day, Guy meets Miriam and she tells him that she wishes to delay the divorce. This disrupts Guy's plans of marrying Anne soon and starting a very important professional project.

Bruno sends Guy a letter in which he invites Guy to visit him and reminds him about the murder plan. Guy feels uncomfortable about the letter and does not respond, but Bruno calls him on the phone and finds out that the divorce has been delayed.

Bruno retaliates by travelling to Metcalf and strangling Miriam to death while Guy is on holiday with Anne.

GUY SURRENDERS TO BRUNO'S PRESSURE

Guy is questioned by the police about Miriam's murder. Although he suspects Bruno might be the murderer, he does not mention him.

Bruno proceeds to harass Guy with letters, telephone calls and unexpected encounters on the street. Guy ignores him, but Bruno issues a warning: if Guy does not kill Bruno's father, Bruno will implicate him in Miriam's murder. Bruno sends him plans to kill his father, including a map of the house and a firearm.

As Guy continues to ignore him, Bruno writes to Anne and to Guy's business partners, telling them he was involved in Miriam's murder. Guy fears his reputation and personal life are being threatened, and starts losing sleep and drinking heavily.

Bruno breaks into Guy's home one night and tells him that the next day will be perfect to murder his father, as Bruno and his mother are going on a trip. Guy decides that the only way to stop this harassment is to do as Bruno says so, following Bruno's plans, Guy shoots Bruno's father in his home. On his escape from the house, he is seen by the family's butler and gets his face scratched from running into bushes.

BRUNO AND GUY GET CLOSER

After the murder, Guy tries to isolate himself but Anne insists on seeing him. She notices the scratches on his face and Guy is forced to lie to her. Anne believes him, and they finally marry.

Feeling increasingly attached to Guy, Bruno invites himself to the wedding and to Anne and Guy's housewarming party. Guy is irritated by this but seems unable to stop Bruno from appearing in his life. They tell everyone that they know each other from school, avoiding mentioning their meeting on the train.

THE DETECTIVE MAKES THE CONNECTIONS

After the murder of Bruno's father, Gerard (the family's personal detective) gets involved in solving the case. He has known Bruno for years and is suspicious of his unstable personality, so he starts interrogating Bruno's friends, including Guy. While investigating Guy, Gerard discovers that Guy's wife (Miriam) has also been murdered. Gerard questions both men about their relationship, and they say that they met each other only a few months ago at a social event, again avoiding mentioning the train encounter.

One day, Bruno suffers from alcohol withdrawal symptoms and, in a delirious dream, he screams Guy's name. Gerard, who is in the house, hears this. While in the house, he also finds the book that Guy left on the train and sees the calls Bruno made to Guy on the days before Miriam's murder. Gerard reaches the conclusion that Bruno plotted exchanging murders with Guy.

Gerard also finds out that Bruno was at Metcalf on the day Miriam was murdered, and gets many witnesses to confirm it. Although he still lacks evidence to prove his point, the detective feels confident that it is only a matter of time before Guy's guilt will make him confess to the murder.

GUY BREAKS DOWN

Gerard decides to interrogate Anne. When Guy gets home, he is forced to lie to Anne again to calm her, which makes him feel even more guilty.

Bruno appears at the couple's home when they are planning to go on a short day trip on their boat, and invites himself. After embarrassing Guy by talking about how special their relationship is, Bruno falls from the boat. Guy jumps into the water but he is unable to find him and Bruno drowns.

With Bruno dead, Guy suddenly feels more isolated and decides to confess. He sets out to tell the truth to Owen Markman, the man Miriam would have married if she had been alive. He travels to Owen's city and manages to get him to listen to him in his hotel room. When he finishes his confession, he receives a call: Gerard has followed him and heard everything through the door. Broken, Guy lets Gerard arrest him.

CHARACTER ANALYSIS

GUY HAINES

Guy Haines is a reputable architect in his late twenties whose career is taking off when the events take place. However, his life is torn apart by his encounter with Bruno and the events that ensue.

From the moment he meets Bruno, he is forced to lead a double life: his ordinary life, in which he is a respectable architect and a loving partner to Anne; and his secret life with Bruno, in which he is blackmailed and stalked until he commits murder. As the plot unfolds, Guy is less and less capable of connecting these two realities. Guy's greatest fear is that his personal life with Anne and his reputation as an architect will be destroyed once the murder is solved.

Because of this double life, Guy navigates duality throughout the book and realises that he is capable both of creating beautiful architectural works, and also of murder.

At the beginning of the book, Guy takes his work very seriously and pursues very ambitious goals. However, after committing murder, he is unable to focus on his work, and stumbles from project to project.

The crime completely destabilises his life and mental health. He feels guilty both about the murder and about leading a secret life and lying to Anne. In fact, he writes many confession documents, only to throw them in the bin. He is sure he will get caught eventually, a thought that makes him paranoid and, at the same time, reassures him because it will prove that the law still applies.

To avoid facing up to the seriousness of his actions, he starts drinking heavily.

He is completely defenceless around Bruno. Although he sees clearly that Bruno is a psychopath and not someone to be trusted, he still lets him manipulate him. He realises Bruno's power to make him act upon his wishes, and thinks about reporting him to the police on several occasions, especially before killing his father. However, when the moment comes, he is never able to confront him.

Once he commits murder, Guy starts trusting Bruno's abilities and plans, and sees it as impossible to think that Bruno will ever get caught.

His physical appearance changes after the crime: his face is covered in scratches which do not go away for many days, and the other characters realise that his face has become even more serious. Looking in the mirror, he sees some white hair.

CHARLES ANTHONY BRUNO

Charles Anthony Bruno is a slender young man in his late twenties (although he is younger than Guy), whose physical appearance gives away his internal mental instability. When Guy meets him on the train, he has got an enormous pimple on his forehead.

He was born into a rich family, acts like a snob and always wants to be the centre of attention. He wants to experiment and to try everything at least once before dying, and believes the rule of law and any other social conventions do not apply to him. He also believes that he is smarter than everyone else, and that neither he nor Guy will ever get caught.

He is shaped by his dysfunctional family relationships and feels a strong hate for his father. He criticises his father's humble origins and the fact that he only married his mother for her fortune.

By contrast, Bruno is emotionally attached to his mother, with a child-like feeling bordering on obsession. He is tremendously possessive when it comes to her, and gets jealous if she has relationships with men.

He is a manipulative man who takes pleasure in making people do whatever he commands, and he is extremely vain and proud. When things do not work according to his plans, he feels betrayed and vulnerable and, in retaliation, he is willing to do anything. His pride and snobbery are portrayed on his trip to Haiti with his mother: when he falls into the water and several cruise employees laugh, he feels extremely humiliated and tries to have the employees fired.

His obsessive personality focuses on a new target when he meets Guy. Bruno becomes infatuated with this ambitious and successful man when he meets him on the train, an obsession he continues to pursue to its final consequences. He loves Guy (a feeling that mixes both brotherly camaraderie and sexual attraction) and wants Guy to feel the same way towards him. In fact, he gets jealous of Anne's relationship to Guy. In his attempts to make Guy like him, Bruno presents him with several expensive gifts, and pretends to be his close friend in front of Guy's personal acquaintances.

His feelings towards Guy change to hate when Guy does not pay attention to him and warns him to stay away. When Bruno kills Miriam, he stalks Guy because he feels like he owes him killing Bruno's father. Bruno feels ecstatic when Guy finally commits the murder. He believes their relationship is now stronger and closer than ever, and unlike any other relationship Guy has with other people.

His interest in murder and crime is awakened by a love for detective novels and true crime stories from the newspapers. However, it is his desire to have control over other people that is most satisfied when he kills.

This is especially true with women. He is a misogynist who classifies women as either saints or prostitutes. He exercises his power over women whenever he can and, after murdering Miriam, he goes on a taxi ride in search for prostitutes.

Bruno feels confident that neither him nor Guy will get caught for the murders, relying on his perfect planning skills and cold blood. However, his obsession with Guy and his unstable personality end up giving away his plans.

This troubled personality is amplified by Bruno's alcohol abuse problems. Throughout the book, he shifts from being extremely inebriated to suffering delusions from alcohol deprivation. In fact, when inebriated, he loses control of his emotions.

ANALYSIS

THE THESIS: CAN ANYONE BECOME A MURDERER?

Bruno has always been fascinated by murder. From the detective novels he has always read to his final act of murder, he sees murder as something he wants to experience before he dies. He has a powerful imagination and, in a way, is disconnected from real life and normal social relationships. Bruno uses this imagination to plot "perfect crimes", where the murderer is never caught. To such a twisted mind, murder seems inevitable. Bruno is also a very controlling person who enjoys making people do what he wants. For him, murder is one more way to control people.

In fact, he believes that anyone can become a murderer. In other words, for Bruno, murder is not just the work of deviant minds, but an action that anyone can perpetrate given the right circumstances.

These ideas are put into practice when he meets Guy. Guy seems to be Bruno's opposite: he is a practical, serious and career-driven man who sees crime as unthinkable. When Bruno mentions murder on the train, the mere thought of it makes him nervous and uncomfortable. However, Bruno manipulates him to the point where Guy ends up committing murder.

In this transition, Guy's life is completely shattered: first, Bruno's harassment forces him to lead a secret life and lie to his family and fiancée. In the process, Bruno increasingly takes control of his thoughts and his world-view, and manages to make the murder seem unavoidable.

After the murder, Guy's guilt makes him isolate himself from the people who love him. He continues to lead two separate lives until he can no longer stand the guilt and he breaks down.

His transformation and his actions prove Bruno's point: anyone can become a murderer.

A CROSS BETWEEN PSYCHOLOGICAL THRILLER AND DETECTIVE STORY

Strangers on a Train's plot combines the characteristics of classic detective stories and the psychological thriller genre.

On the one hand, the novel draws many of its characteristics from the genre of psychological thrillers:

it focuses on the characters' psychological delusions and stress, which lead them to perpetrate evil and crime. This is typical of psychological thrillers, which focus on the characters' twisted thoughts and anxieties.

In *Strangers on a Train*, this is visible in both characters. Bruno's evident lunacy and obsessive behaviour are classic character traits that tend to be explored by psychological thrillers. Moreover, Highsmith is particularly interested in portraying Guy's transition from an upright man to a murderer, and how this process makes him paranoid and isolated.

Furthermore, both characters in *Strangers on a Train* display a sense of delusion and seem to have problems grasping reality. This is also commonly explored in psychological thrillers. On the one hand, Bruno is detached from reality from the beginning of the novel, as we can see from details like his lack any normal social relationships (like friends) and his constant escape from reality through alcohol. Guy, on the other hand, becomes increasingly delusional as Bruno's manipulation takes hold of him. His lack of sleep and drinking habits accentuate his inability to think straight.

Furthermore, in both *Strangers on a Train* and other psychological thrillers, the action is less important than describing the characters' minds and their train of thought. The narrator emphasises the characters' inner thoughts as propellers for their actions. In fact, in *Strangers on a Train*, there are some outside actions whose purpose is to show how anxious the character is feeling (for instance, when Guy is unable to sleep on the days before the murder, or when Bruno suffers from delusional dreams).

However, the novel also incorporates some elements drawn from classic detective stories.

For instance, both *Strangers on a Train* and other detective stories incorporate a skilful detective who manages to solve a mysterious crime thanks to their wit and clear intuition. In this regard, Gerard is a classic detective, who works independently and manages to solve two murders that have kept the police disoriented.

Classic detective stories are also usually based on the idea of a perfect crime that seems impossible to solve. In fact, as is made clear in the novel, Bruno gets his idea about exchanging murders after having been obsessed with detective stories all his life.

The ability of chance and coincidences to completely overturn lives is also explored in *Strangers on a Train* and other detective stories. Indeed, chance and coincidences play a very important role in the novel: Guy's life is completely transformed by his chance encounter with Bruno on the train, and the book that Guy leaves in Bruno's compartment is found by Gerard by chance, thus enabling him to progress in his investigation.

DUALITY AS THE NATURE OF EVERYTHING

The novel is constructed around duality on a number of different levels.

First of all, it involves two characters and explores the way their lives become entangled as a result of a chance encounter. These two characters initially represent two very different, almost diametrically opposed, personalities: Guy is a serious, hard-working and self-contained man, while Bruno is lazy and selfish and has obvious problems with drinking and problematic social relationships. Guy falls in love with women and Bruno despises women. Guy's mind is practical, while Bruno is imaginative and twisted.

The two men meet on a train and their relationship evolves into duality, so that they both end up feeling love and hate for each other, being enemies and accomplices at the same time.

This duality is also explored on a philosophical level, especially through the character of Guy. As the novel progresses, Guy reflects on how he has both the power of creation (in his architectural work) and the power of destruction (murder).

Guy moves on to think about how every man and woman possesses duality within themselves: love and hate, positive and negative, artistic genius and foolishness... He contemplates how nothing exists without its opposite.

In the end, Guy reaches the conclusion that, just as electrons and neutrons live together inside the atom, good and evil live together inside every human.

FURTHER REFLECTION

SOME QUESTIONS TO THINK ABOUT...

- Watch Alfred Hitchcock's film adaptation of the novel. What are the main changes he introduced in the plot?
- Hitchcock decided to change the novel's ending for his *Strangers on a Train* film. Discuss whether his ending is more effective than Highsmith's and the reasons why he might have done this.
- Read Highsmith's *The Talented Mr. Ripley*. Compare Bruno and Tom Ripley, the two psychopaths created by Highsmith, and discuss whether they share any characteristics.
- Consider how Guy's perception of Bruno evolves throughout the book, from thinking he is a harmless lunatic, to being manipulated by him and hating him, to trying to save his life. Make a note of particular scenes or plot twists that play a key role in transforming this relationship.

- Explore how Bruno's harassment, combined with his mellow manners, is able to finally take control over Guy's life. Make a note of particular scenes that illustrate Bruno's hold over Guy.
- Analyse the female characters in *Strangers on a Train*. Discuss what type of role they play in the novel, and whether they demonstrate any independence from their male companions.
- Highsmith struggled to cope with her sexual attraction for other women, and felt this forced her to lead a double life. Analyse how this conflict is explored through Guy's double life after he meets Bruno.
- Bruno's feelings towards Guy have often been compared to sexual attraction. Find evidence of Bruno's attraction to Guy in the novel.

We want to hear from you!
Leave a comment on your online library
and share your favourite books on social media!

FURTHER READING

REFERENCE EDITION

- Highsmith, P. (1988) *Strangers on a Train*. London: Penguin Books.

REFERENCE STUDIES

- Hart, K. (2011) The Inner Life of Patricia Highsmith. *This Recording*. [Online]. [Accessed 22 November 2018]. Available from: <http://thisrecording.com/today/2011/8/15/in-which-patricia-highsmith-endures-a-depression-equal-to-he.html>

ADDITIONAL SOURCES

- Highsmith, P. (2001) *Plotting and Writing Suspense Fiction.* London: St. Martins Griffin.
- Wilson, A. (2010) *Beautiful Shadow: A Life of Patricia Highsmith*. London: Bloomsbury.

ADAPTATIONS

- *Strangers on a Train.* (1951) [Film]. Alfred Hitchcock Dir. USA: Warner Bros.

MORE FROM BRIGHTSUMMARIES.COM

- Reading guide – *The Talented Mr. Ripley* by Patricia Highsmith.

www.brightsummaries.com

Ebook EAN: 9782808015677

Paperback EAN: 9782808015684

Legal Deposit: D/2018/12603/542

Cover: © Primento

Digital conception by Primento, the digital partner of publishers.